Haifa

and Other Poems

by

Samih Masoud

Translated and Edited by
Nizar Sartawi

inner child press, ltd.

Credits

Author

Samih Masoud

Editor

Nizar Sartawi

Translator

Nizar Sartawi

Cover Design

Inner Child Press

General Information

Haifa and other poems

Samih Masoud

1st Edition : May 2016

This Publishing is protected under Copyright Law as a "Collection". All rights for all submissions are retained by the Individual Artist and / or Poet. No part of this Publishing may be Reproduced, Transferred in any manner without the prior **WRITTEN CONSENT** of the "Material Owner" or it's Representative Inner Child Press. Any such violation infringes upon the Creative and Intellectual Property of the Owner pursuant to International and Federal Copyright Law. Any queries pertaining to this "Collection" should be addressed to Publisher of Record.

Publisher Information

1st Edition : Inner Child Press, Ltd.
innerchildpress@gmail.com
www.innerchildpress.com

This Collection is protected under U.S. and International Copyright Laws.

Copyright © 2016

ISBN-13 : 978-0692703793

ISBN-10 : 0692703799

$ 16.95

Table of Contents

Preface   7
Introduction   9

Haifa and other poems   23

Where Are You From?	25
For Whom The Bell Tolls	26
A Wanderer	29
I Am Here	30
Haifa	31
What Binds Together?	34
Forough Farrokhzad	37
The City Of Stars	41
Why?	43
The Lady OF The Highest Balcony	44
Jerusalem	48
Two Immigrants	50
Remnants Of Days	53
Who Is Like You?	57
Where Am I, Where Are You?	58

Table of Contents ... *continued*

An Arab Woman	59
Death Is Chasing Me	60
Why Have You Come Here?	61
He Said To Her	63
The Mirage Of Memories	65
Faces In The Crowd	66
Tango	67

Epilogue 69

About The Author	71
Samih Masoud's Web Links	73
About The Editor / Translator	75

Preface

The poems in this collection are a reflection of visions and feelings that spring from my experience as a poet who has been driven away from his country – who coups with the hardships of life in the diaspora by reminiscing about his homeland on all occasions, nourishing his love of humanity, and expressing his support of the oppressed all over the world both directly and symbolically, through his poetry.

In composing these poems I have been stimulated by my strong and intimate ties with my birthplace, Haifa, the city which occupies my mind and heart all the time – the city I bear like a tattoo in my eyes and heart. The poems are filled with pictures driven from my childhood days and my dreams about my homeland. My bond with Haifa remains a constant source of emotional and spiritual inspiration. And that is why the book bears its name.

I must acknowledge the great effort exerted by my friend, poet Nizar Sartawi, one of the outstanding Arab translators, who has encouraged me to have my book published. With his sincere friendship and full, unconditional support, he has been instrumental in ensuring that the work be accomplished. I owe him for all that he has done.

Samih Masoud

Introduction

*Longing and Belonging :
The Sense of Place in Masoud's Poetry*

I carried Beir Zeit for absence
an olive tree, a rock
a home
and a raining tear that
brings heaven closer

~ Adeeb Naser, *I am Searching for Me*

How painful it is to mourn, sing for, or even talk about a lost homeland! One unforgettable incident that I witnessed was when Samih Masoud ascended the platform to speak about his autobiographical book *Haifa Burqa – A Search for Roots* (2013).[1] Masoud's speech was part of a two-day event organized by The Jordanian Writers Association. The title of the event was "Returning

---

[1] Burqa, the town Masoud's grandparents came from, is a Palestinian town located 18 kilometers northwest of Nablus. Haifa, is Masoud's birthplace; it is a major Palestinian coastal city on the Mediterranean Sea, built on the slopes of Mount Carmel.

To Haifa." It was held in Al-Hussein Cultural Center in Amman on May 24 – 25, 2014.

Masoud stood behind the microphone to present his book. Recalling his first return to Haifa in 1995, after 47 years of absence, he said:

"We [Masoud and his companions] went up to Mar Elias Monastery[2] on top of *Mount Carmel*, overlooking Haifa. We ascended a little hill near the monastery. I stood there and looked around for a while, filling my eyes with the magnificent landscape. Suddenly I found myself shouting at the top of my voice: 'Haifa is here/ I am here/ The sea gathers us/ hand in hand/ with the almond/ the olive/ and the moon above'"[3]

Overcome with emotion, Masoud fell silent for a while. He pulled a napkin from his pocket and wiped his eyes. Apparently, it was a grave moment for the 74-year-old man – the man who had spent most of his life in the Diaspora dreaming of coming back to his homeland. Later that afternoon, a lady from the audience approached him and said: "You made us cry today." And *yes he did*.

---

[2] Mar Elias Monastry, also known as The Stella Maris Monastery or The Monastery of Our Lady of Mount Carmel in Haifa is located on the slopes of Mount Carmel.

[3] This incident is recounted in detail in *Haifa Burqa – The Search for the Roots*, pp. 191-92.

~ ~ ~

The Mar Elis encounter not only reveals the depth and intensity of Masoud's passion and longing for his motherland, it also points to the most prominent feature in his poetry, namely his attachment to the *place*. For him the place is a gigantic store of memories that enrich his content – a rich mine from which he derives his topics or draws material for his poems. As Hanne observed, for some writers living in exile the "subject matter [is] exclusively linked to the place... they have been cut off from" (8). [4]

In fact, Masoud's intimate attachment to the place is markedly reflected in most of his poems. Looking at the list of contents in this book, we cannot fail to see how the sense of place is predominant even in poem titles, such as "Jerusalem," "Haifa," "The City O Stars," "Where Are You From?," "A Wanderer," "I Am Here," "Where Am I, Where Are You?," "Why Have You Come Here?" As we peruse the book, we notice how Masoud uses a lot of common nouns referring to places, like sea, city, village, mountain, hell, home, house, church, mosque, grove, and so on. We also come across a large number of proper

---

[4] Hanne, Michael. *Creativity In Exile*. New York: odopi, 2004.

11

nouns – names of cities, villages, and other places, including Haifa, Jerusalem, Askalan, Iskal, Cana, Jlaim, Wadi Nisnas, the Hadar, Mount Carmel.

With the exception of Jerusalem and Askalan, these places, it must be noted, are located in the Galilee, north of Palestine, where Masoud spent his early childhood. They were engraved in his mind and heart. Despite the *Nakba* – the displacement and dispossession of most Arab-Palestinians following the 1948 war – the wistful memories of those days remained with the ten-year-old boy all his life, brightening his dreams and fueling his undying nostalgia. Thus he writes in his poem about the city of "Haifa:" "Never do I forget where my home was/ I bear it as a tattoo in the eye along the paths of my diaspora."

~ ~ ~

A careful examination of Masoud's poems reveals that the kind of attachment connecting him with the place largely depends on its geographical location, or setting, particularly whether it is in Palestine or in the Diaspora.

In the poems set in the diaspora, Masoud's emotional connection to the place is virtually nonexistent. Although the poet seems to attach importance to many of the places that he mentions or describes, he obviously sees them with the eye of a newcomer. What these poems really focus on is the poet's status as an immigrant who has been forced to leave his homeland and live in exile. Reading them, we cannot miss the feeling of estrangement and loss of identity or the waves of nostalgia sweeping through them.

Thus while the diasporic poem may mostly be about an afternoon walk in a street or part of a city, we discover at the end that the poet's mind is elsewhere, and that, despite the seemingly strong interest in this or that site, he actually feels like a wanderer walking aimlessly in a place where he does not belong. Then the memories of his lost homeland are evoked, and he realizes that his life has become somewhat empty and meaningless.

This can be clearly observed in three diasporic poems in which the poet's ambulatory *tours* are recounted: "For Whom the Bell Tolls," "Two Immigrants," and "Remnants of Days." The first poem is set in Chicago, the second and third in Montreal. In these poems the poet mentions a number of well-known places or sites that meet his eyes along the way: Oak Park, River Forest, and Harlem Avenue in the first poem; La Fayette, Champlain Bridge, Saint Laurent river, Notre Dame, and Raucous corners in the second; Berri-

UQAM, Westmount, De Maisonneuve, and Maison de Jazz in the third.

Although these tours suggest that the poet has a strong interest in places in general, this interest, has no emotional weight. It seems to spring mainly from his curiosity – his propensity for exploration and discovery. In this sense he is more like a photographer who takes snapshots of the scenes that catch his eye. Otherwise, his attachment to these places tends to be casual and transitory. Once his contact with them is over, he lapses into a state of estrangement and a sense of lack of identity.

This is exactly what happens in each of the three poems. "For Whom the Bell Tolls," for example, concludes with bewildered, "deathly silence:"

For whom The Bells Toll?
For you?
For him?
For her?
For me?
Who is shrouded in deathly silence
at sunset?

In the closing lines of "Two Immigrants," a mixture of estrangement and nostalgia dominates the scene:

And here you

and I now
are walking, two immigrant strangers
in the exiles of the diaspora
our dreams overflowing around us
looking for rainy clouds
to bring back the pulse
to the migrant
birds.

And in "Remnants of Days." The voice of a woman singing "Strangers" brings back the memories. A sense of loss is experienced by the poet and "I go again back to the roads."

In other poems with a diasporic setting, feelings of estrangement and nostalgia become so intense that the place loses its significance almost entirely. Instead, the focus is on the psychological state of the poet, who, away from his homeland, pictures himself as a lonely, depressed person or a desperate wanderer – a disconsolate soul that has lost the sense of purpose in life. Thus in "Why Have You Come Here?" he falls into a fit of self-reproach:

Why have you come here
to places that are not yours
wandering
among the footmarks
of paths

forgetting your shadow
in the seasons of
migration?

In "A Wanderer" the poet is alone in a devastated vessel stricken by the waves while the memories of "the days of youth" pass in his mind. In "The Mirage of Memories" he sinks into a state of total despair. "We're both finished," he tells his beloved. "Our days are lost/ and all that was is gone."

~ ~ ~

While poems with a diasporic setting express feelings of alienation and nostalgia, poems set in Palestine express a strong sense of belonging. It is worth noting that belonging in these poems is often expressed in the possessive mode. Therefore, words like *my* and *our*, known in grammar as *possessives* are used extensively to affirm ownership of the land of Palestine by the Arab Palestinians, thus responding implicitly to the Jewish claims to it. For example, in his poem, "What Binds Us Together?" Masoud writes:

We're bound together
by the land of Canaan
...
We're bound together
by our mountains

rocks
hills
houses
furrows
groves
and palm
fronds

In "Where Are You From?" the title serves as a hypothetical question which the poet answers directly and assertively:

I'm from here
My mother is here
My father is here
My family too
and this sea
is my own
I am his waves
and his spray.
I'm from here
My house has been here
for a thousand
years

Similarly, Masoud emphasizes the Palestinian people's right to the land in "Why" by asking: "Why/ do they steal *our* land/ *our* soil/ trees/ churches/ mosques/ and all that belongs to us?" (emphasis added).

In other poems this possessiveness becomes more profound, taking a spiritual form. Spiritual connection according to Cross[5] is emotional in nature. A person who is spiritually tied to a place feels "a sense of belonging," which the writer describes as intangible. In Masoud's poetry, however, the spiritual bond is much deeper than sheer belonging. At times it becomes like a vision or a dream in which he sees his homeland in objects or people that have some connection with it. In "He Said to Her," for example, the poet sees Palestine, or at least part of it, in the eyes of a woman, evidently because she is a Palestinian:

in your eyes I see
a land
stretching further and further
from Haifa to Askalan
I see our sea
our trees
almonds
olives
wild flowers
and anemones

Elsewhere, the bond with the place tends to take a religious form in which the poet's feelings are so

---

[5] Cross, Jennifer E. "What is Sense of Place?" 12th Headwaters Conference, Western State College, November, 2001. Web. 10 September 2014.
http://western.edu/sites/default/files/documents/cross_headwatersXII.pdf

intense that they transform into something like worship. "Haifa" is perhaps the poem in which such tendency is best illustrated. It begins with the moment when the poet meets his *beloved* city:

O my eternal love
Lo! I come back to you again
on the wings of clouds
Lo! I'm here with you
I tuck my heart into your beach
and forget the remote exiles

As the poem progresses, the city becomes more like a goddess whose "tresses rise... above the passageways of heaven," and from whose "tender bosom... the threads of light emerge..." Then comes the moment when he arrives at his home. Now the home turns into a holy shrine, or rather a Kaaba, where worship rituals are performed: "When I get there I drop my face on its thresholds/ I kiss it and go around it seven times *and more*" (emphasis added). Here the poem reaches the climax with what is probably one of the most emotional experiences in Masoud's life.

~ ~ ~

When Masoud and his family were uprooted from their home and homeland in 1948, he was barely ten years of age. Ever since he has been living in the Diaspora. Apart from the sporadic visits which he has had the opportunity to make to Palestine since 1995, he has spent his life dreaming of Palestine. Thus the world for him has been divided into two places: The homeland and the Diaspora. And it is the homeland that has occupied both his mind and heart.

Masoud's poetry can mostly be regarded as a reflection of his life. It is hardly possible to draw a line of demarcation between the two – to separate the persona, or the voice in the poems, from the man himself. Masoud has experienced feelings of estrangement and nostalgia in the Diaspora; he has felt an undying passion and yearning for his homeland. And it is these feelings, these sentiments of longing and belonging that figure predominantly in his poetry.

for

Haifa,

the birthplace of my dreams.

Haifa

and other poems

Haifa and other poems

Samih Masoud

Where Are You From?

I'm from here
My mother is here
My father is here
My family too
and this sea
is my own
I am his waves
and his spray.
I'm from here
My house has been here
for a thousand
years
a thousand years
These are its stones
like clouds
with a thousand doors
a thousand doors

Do you now know
who I am?
I'm from here
from the soil of Haifa
My house is here
It will remain
it will remain

Haifa and other poems

For Whom The Bell Tolls? [6]

I am here in
your ancient house
watching the graffiti and papers
from the days of your youth
Tell me
For whom do you think
the bells toll
in Oak Park? [7]
For you or her?
You are here
Maria is here
She passes hurriedly with a shy
eye
a red band on
her loosened hair
matching her complexion
and saddles
swaggering around her
lighting the stars
Behold, I hear her voice

---

6 This is the title of Ernest Hemingway's novel, published in 1940, which is based on his experiences during the Spanish Civil War. The protagonist, Robert Jordan, is an American who fights with Spanish soldiers for the Republicans.

7 Oak Park is a village adjacent to the western side of the city of Chicago in Cook County, Illinois, United States.

ringing aloud
she sings Hallelujah
in her melodious voice
Here I see Lorca
passing by her
with bleeding feet
I follow him
from one street to another
as he rides on the saddle
of River Forest[8]
At the sliding of
Harlem Avenue[9]
he vanishes and disappears
and the bleeding moon
comes into view once and again and disappears
vanishes in the shadow and disappears
and then appears again.

~ ~ ~

I leave it now
I go back again
to your home in the same place
drawn by your heavy bells
And I ask the question
all over again

---

[8] River Forest is a suburban village in Cook County, Illinois, United States.
[9] Harlem Avenue is a major street in Chicago.

For whom The Bell Toll?
For you?
For him?
For her?
For me?
Who is shrouded in deathly silence
at sunset?

A Wanderer

Wandering
The waves strike
against the remnants of my vessel
Alone I go
with the shadow of your face
by my side.
Along the paths
emerge the days of youth
in our land
our kin
our homes
and all that was ours
almonds and olives
and mijana[10]

---

10 mijana, is a form of the Palestinian folk music tradition.

I am Here

Haifa[11]
is here
I am here
The sea gathers us
hand in hand
with the almond
the olive
and the moon above

~ ~ ~

Haifa is here
I am here
I come to you today
as a pilgrim

~ ~ ~

For sixty years
I've waited for this day
Sixty years have passed
till my hair turned grey.

---

11 Poet's place of birth from which he was displaced by force only to return sixty years later, but as a foreigner.

Haifa

O my eternal love
Lo! I come back to you again
on the wings of clouds
Lo! I'm here with you
I tuck my heart into your beach
and forget the remote exiles
I spell every part of you
the sea, the waves, the wind and the trees
the dew's whispers in the morning
the winter spouts
and mirrors hanging on the wings of the wind
laden with tapes of scenic memories
that bring the heartbeats back to the heart in the crowded life
and take me back to the past
In them I see all that I want to see
the quivering of my bygone days
sites loosened from the prophets' faces
around which I go
morning and evening
O my city
Whose tresses rise akin to yours above the passageways of heaven,
and a tender bosom wherefrom the threads of light emerge?

Haifa and other poems

O my city
Whenever I come to you, my pride and passion soar
I go into your mirrors as your waves wish me to
Never do I forget where my home was
I bear it as a tattoo in the eye along the paths of my diaspora
When I get there I drop my face on its thresholds
I kiss it and go around it seven times and more
From hidden nooks I gather the relics my mother left
laden with the sweetest memories
I breathe in the breeze of life
In its surroundings I hear my mother's melodious voice trembling
It never loses me
It follows me
awakens me
I see my mother
hugging me with her large bright eyes
hiding me in her eyes
her smile emerging as wide as the space
Here mother quivered on an olden day
And I started crawling
Here I saw her
I spelled her face with love and affection
Lo! I've come to my house again
after years
and years

It is my joy
my desired passion
My heart flutters around it
goes deep into sorrows
I feel in its odor all that has passed
I go back
putting together the faces of those who had been here
and then were lost in the paths of humiliation
I weave sails
to extend for the them in the whole place
With these I fill my dreams and bring them back
to the lap of Haifa
with the steps of a wild wind
that lingers not.

What Binds Us Together?

We're bound together
by the land of Canaan
A thousand thousand years
of a long
past

~ ~ ~

We're bound together
by our mountains
rocks
hills
houses
furrows
groves
and palm
fronds

~ ~ ~

We're bound together
by cyclamen
narcissus
and quitch grass

~ ~ ~

We're bound together
by Iksal[12]
Cana[13]

and all the villages
of Galilee

~ ~ ~

We're bound together
by a wave dancing with
Haifa
in the forenoon
and before
sunset

~ ~ ~

We're bound together
by our history
before exile
and after exile

~ ~ ~

---

12 Iskal is a town in northern Palestine about 5 kilometers southeast of Nazareth.

13 Cana is a town in northern Palestine eight kilometers northeast of Nazareth.

We're bound together
by ataba
mijana
oaff
and original
zajal[14]

~ ~ ~

We're bound together
by our tents
and hopes
for an approaching beautiful
morrow

---

14 Ataba, mijana, oaff, and zajal are forms of the Palestinian folk music tradition.

Forough Farrokhzad[15]

I met your lovers
in Tehran
I asked them about your heartbeats
the strings of your rhymes
(roaring with fire and compassion)
and your remote shelter
in the sunset
on the banks of the Karun[16]

and your blissful steps
on beaches
I asked them about your hair, strewn about
without a chador[17]
your short
sleeveless dress
They spoke to me of the temples
of love
the warmth of your heart
at the moment of perception
in the evening

---

15 Forugh Farrokhzād 1935 – 1967) is considered one of Iran's most influential female poets of the twentieth century.

16 The Karun is the largest river in Iran.

17 A chador is an outer garment or open cloak worn by many Iranian women and female teenagers in public spaces.

and the blue
rain showers of your clouds

~ ~ ~

I met my friend Hafez Shirazi[18]
in Shiraz
I asked him about you
He sang a stanza of yours
about love and man
He spoke to me of the "Rebellion" poem
about a little bird
that had flown towards the bright
skies of poetry
He spoke to me of the
"Captive"
of long embracing
arms

~ ~ ~

One evening
he spoke to me
of the "Sin" poem
Nodding his head
He recited it bashfully

---

18 Khwaja Shamsu d-Din Muhammad Hafez-e Shirazi, known by his pen name Hafez, was a famous fourteenth century Persian poet.

and drank a few glasses
of wine so passionately

~ ~ ~

One summer day
O my friend
I walked along the alleyways of Tehran
I went to your address
In the same spot,
Zahir-od-dowleh Cemetery[19],

I found around you garlands of flowers
women, men
and young ones
lighting candles
after candles
In their midst
a woman reciting the loveliest poems
and around her
all were singing
singing

---

19 Zahir-od-dowleh Cemetery is located in Darband within the city limits of Tehran. Many great Iranian artists, poets, and thinkers are buried there.

Haifa and other poems

Eyes met
And met again
I asked about you
Everybody said
with a high pitched voice
that filled the ears:
This is the shrine of Farrokhzad
the lady of poetry and poets

The City Of Stars

This is the city of stars
brimming with dew and lights
her tresses ascending above the domes of heaven
her waves fluttering
in perpetual dance
There, you're within her now
listening to her melodious voice
in the evening
You sleep and wake up
to the memories of the place

There, you're within her now
dressed in wounds
wandering among the shelves of memories
collecting from your bygone yesterday
all that has passed
fragments
ornamented
with Wadi Nisnas[20]

Jlaim[21]

---

20 Wadi Nisnas is an Arab neighborhood in the occupied city of Haifa in northern Palestine.
21 Jlaim is a beach in Haifa

Haifa and other poems

The Carmel[22]
the sea
the Hadar[23]

and the thirsty trees
of your house.

---

22 The Carmel is a coastal mountain range in northern Palestine stretching from the Mediterranean Sea towards the southeast.

23 Hadar is a neighborhood of Haifa located on the northern slope of Mount Carmel between the upper and lower city.

Why?

Why
do they steal our land
our soil
trees
churches
mosques
and all that belongs to us?

~ ~ ~

Why are the prayers banned
in our Jerusalem?
Why do they build a wall around us?
Why is Abraham
theirs and ours,
their grandfather and ours,
and they are our cousins?

~ ~ ~

Who said he was here?
Who said they lived here
in the innards
of our history?

The Lady Of The Highest Balcony

She wrote to him; "I might send you some light with the sea wind passing through my balcony on the heights of the Carmel"

There
she slumbers on the shoulders of
Haifa...
her wicks wearing the light
of the day...
her fiddle filling the Carmel
singing loud
its echo ringing in far-off
isles.
The waves leap around her
scorching the blue of the sea
their breezes coming for her
with the rise of the morning
loosening her braids
shadows for the moon

~ ~ ~

I see her
wandering aboard the expanding waves

drawing a painting wet
with the almond blossoms
and punches of grapes

~ ~ ~

My lady
Draw me
on Haifa's
beach
carrying figs and thyme

~ ~ ~

Reconstruct my face
full of days long past
without a smile
for I don't know laughter
I lost it
in the gloomy days
of my wandering

~ ~ ~

Draw me
on Haifa's
beach
kneeling on its sand
Fill my eyes with it

Haifa and other poems

~ ~ ~

Paste its breeze
in my veins
Wrap me with a Palestinian
bright blue
qumbaz[24]

~ ~ ~

Do not give a name
to my portrait
I lost my name
in the paths of my Diaspora
Write:
This is Haifa's
lover

In his very eye
he holds her
and hides her
he's never been away from her
he still lives there
a root in
her hills

~ ~ ~

---

[24] The qumbaz is a Palestinian traditional dress for men.

O lady
of the highest balcony
Leave it open
Let Haifa's breeze
pass through it
wrapped with dew…

Keep singing
from there to the farthest reaches

~ ~ ~

Leave it
open
that my wandering
sails
may gaze at her

Jerusalem

O Jerusalem
City of peace
Your little children
are crucified
morning and evening
and your women
die in their deep grief
O Jerusalem
Hymns are not heard
in your ancient house
Prayers are not allowed
in the prophets' houses
Their bells are pigmented with blood
No water
No air
No fire
No light
The candles are turned off
The stars are stolen
in the threshing floors of heaven
O Jerusalem
No matter how long we suffer
and taste the pains of misery
we will always be here
growing like thorns in the eyes of strangers
we will remain inside you
growing olives

almonds
and chestnuts
tell the tales of our grandfathers
around the fire brazier
in the winter nights
sing ataba
play the fiddle every evening
dance the dabka[25]
as we please
and reap wheat
when July arrives.
We stay in you
in your hamlets
the symbols of pride
Within the twinkle of an eye
a thousand baby boys are born
a thousand baby girls
a thousand poems
and caravans
of martyrs and poets.

~ ~ ~

O Jerusalem
O icon of glory
in the heights of heaven

---

[25] A folk dance native to the Levant.

Two Immigrants

We arrived at Avenue Greene in the afternoon
The Montréal sun, as always in July,
wore his bright tresses
loosened with combs of flame
we sat at La Fayette
his coffee was boiling
on firewood cinders
We sat
you and I
retold our tales
drank coffee

and sneered
at the fiascos of Arab leaders.

~ ~ ~

At length
we went out
and roamed
from one place
to another
Behold we're now
near Champlain

Bridge
I stroll around it
here
with stiff knees
as you walk beside me

swaying your glowing bosom
with poise
hiding the sun
from the banks
of Saint Laurent
and the bells s
of Notre Dame

~ ~ ~

We walked on
and on
beneath switched off lights
Behold, we've arrived at
Raucous corners
that humor people
with songs and innocent
merriment
The night never leaves them
nor does the morning rise

~ ~ ~

Haifa and other poems

We walked
towards a memorial
riding above the shelves of the wind
Lo! We are beside it now
gazing at a bygone age
counting the faces of those who
passed
from here before us
the old conquering strangers
and good old
Mohawk and Cree Indians
Here they came before us

millenniums ago
filling Montréal's
horizon and space.

~ ~ ~

And here you
and I now
are walking, two immigrant strangers
in the exiles of the diaspora
our dreams overflowing around us
looking for rainy clouds
to bring back the pulse
to the migrant
birds.

Remnants Of Days

All alone
on the thresholds of UQAM[26]
Nothing around save
the spray
of days
shaking within me
traveling in the circles
of the place.
Days
days
loosened from dew
and anemone flowers.
Do you know
I'm counting them now?
One day
two days
filled with her perfume
I wander
following her track
from one place
to another.
I follow her
I race with her

---

26 Berri-UQAM is the central station of the Montréal Metro system.

the peal of my feet thundering
behind her here
and there.
I move quickly
along the roads
Here is Westmount
awake with the night
To her I come and she to me.
De Maisonneuve is before my eyes
expanding before my steps
I walk through it silently
No one is there but I.
I walk
and walk
endlessly.
Here is Maison
de Jazz
emerging in the dark of the night
belted with lights
Five names it has.
I see it and it sees me
now.
I remember a woman
who was there
one evening.
She swayed in ecstasy

as she sang.
I lost her
Who can
bring her back
as I desire?
I step inside now
close my eyes
and hear
"Strangers"
in the voice
of a dark woman
singing
singing long.
Between one song and another
memories take me unawares
I go again back to the roads.
Lo! I'm moving
again
with the winds
running after those days
running
and gasping
in the wide space.
I roam
and the gasping wind
rises up in my chest.
I count the days again

Haifa and other poems

Do you know?
I'm counting them now
One day
Two days
Two
I feel them from a distance
I see them hidden
in the labyrinths of absence
fragments being spilled
in the mirrors of mirage.
With them I spell
all that
was.
I draw the alphabets
around them
with a quiver
laden with questions, one
after another

Who are you O ma'am
for me to stay in the orbits of your eyes
without shadows
wandering alone
whispering to the winds,
lightening and mountains
to say what may be said
and what may not
and forget my insomnia in Montreal.

Who Is Like You?

The stars are drunken
As they float around you
in every direction
to you they come
in the wing of the night
as they please
bringing you light
Who among women
is your peer
in whose track the stars follow
morning and evening
taking pride in her
sprinkling in her bosom
the light of heaven?

Where am I, Where Are You?

Where am I, where are you?
So enchanting are your lips
from them trickles wine
So wide and beautiful are your eyes
so dreamy
in them the moon does shine
The tresses of your hair
are full of charm
Perfume from them flows
your bosom below them dances

Where am I, where are you?
Time has dealt me so

An Arab woman

She has Arab
eyes
cheeks
and lips
Her mouth is a red
ruby.
Her pretty face
lights
the stars.
On her fingers
henna dances.
On her braids
are anemone flowers
and other things
On the curve of her bosom
lights prance.

A belle
whose peer
I've never seen
A belle!

Death Is Chasing Me

Death has been chasing me
for thirty years
drawing his blinds
detaining me in his hands
I listen to him
see his face with my own eyes
and sip from his glass
little
by little.
I go round him
I shake his hand
and in
the morning
he leaves me
disappears from my sight
and on the edge of a gasp
the moment goes on
digging out the ash of wounds
deep inside.

Why Have You Come Here?

Why have you come here?
beyond the oceans
wandering
in the hidden corners of the long
winter?
rubbing your eyes
in the flow
of snow
tracking the steps of the winds
in your dark nights.
You walk on two weary

worn out legs
in the depths of the dark.

~ ~ ~

There you are
fully dressed in rags
immersed in
the mud of the paths
You glide into bars
with open doors
where you enjoy luscious drinks
in large glasses

so large
you gulp one glass
then another
and come back in
the morning
low-voiced
absent-minded
abhorring your hollow
self.
You come back to
your rusty
room
gaze with wandering eyes
at old, forgotten
newspapers.

~ ~ ~

Why have you come here
to places that are not yours
wandering
among the footmarks
of paths
forgetting your shadow
in the seasons of
migration?

Samih Masoud

He Said To Her

He said to her:
in your eyes I see
a land
stretching further and further
from Haifa to Askalan[27]
I see our sea
our trees
almonds
olives
wild flowers
and anemones

~ ~ ~

I see
our children
elders
women
martyrs
houses
sky
air
and flint stones

~ ~ ~

---

[27] Askalan is a Palestinian city located to the north of Gaza Strip on the Mediterranean coast.

I see
all that was once ours
in the mirrors
of time.

The Mirage Of Memories

I take you back to the orbits of an echo
and we meet in the mirage
of a bygone day
We meet
But I am not myself
and you are other than her
whom I used to see
We're both finished
Our days are lost
and all that was
is gone.

Faces In The Crowd

In your eyes you carry
faces
that you move to the whole
world
You paint them
above high stars
You stretch them to
the farthest corners of exile
You grope with them
for poetry
in the long night
and spread them
on the palm fronds
dazzled in the quiet of the night
You meet them and the singing goes on and on
For two days you gulp the greeting glass.
Then comes the parting
and you remain a stranger
in the farthest ends of space
you sail through the little window
with no companions.

Tango

Will you dance
my friend?
Will you dance?
Tango
Do you know how to dance it?
Do you?
One step forward
two steps to the left
and right
and two steps
back
with ease
to the rhythm
of the quivering hands
and the whisper
of lips
and eyes.

Haifa and other poems

epilogue

Haifa and other poems ~ Samih Masoud

Samih Masoud

about the Author...

Samih Masoud is a poet, writer, and researcher. He was born in Haifa, Palestine, in 1938. He studied economics at Sarajevo University and received his Bachelor's degree in 1963. He then received his Master's degree from Belgrade University in 1965, and Ph.D. from the same university in 1967.

In addition to his work in economics, including his two-volume *Encyclopedia of Economics* and 12 other books, Masoud published one poetry collection, one book on literature, and his autobiographical work, *Haifa... Burqa: A Search for Roots*. Also many of his poems and articles have appeared in literary magazines and newspapers.

Masoud is a member of the Jordanian Writers Association.

He is also a co-founder and chairperson of the Canadian Center for Middle Eastern Studies (CMESC) and Al- Andalus Cultural Salon, a cultural branch of CMESC. The salon hosts gatherings of poets and writers and it publishes books in Arabic, English, and French.

Masoud lives with his family between Montréal, Canada and Amman, Jordan.

Samih Masoud's
Web Links

Web Site

www.samihmasoud.com/

FaceBook

www.facebook.com/samih.masoud

Nizar Sartawi

about *Nizar Sartawi* ...

Editor and Translator

Nizar Sartawi is a poet, translator and educator. He was born in Sarta, Palestine, in 1951. He holds a Bachelor's degree in English Literature from the University of Jordan, Amman, and a Master's degree in Human Resources Development from the University of Minnesota, the U.S. Sartawi is a member of the Jordanian Writers Association, General Union of Arab Writers, and Asian-African Writers Union. He has participated in poetry readings and festivals in Jordan, Lebanon, Morocco, Kosovo, and Palestine.

Sartawi's first poetry collection, **Between Two Eras**, was published in Beirut, Lebanon in 2011. His translations include: **The Prayers of the Nightingale** (2013), poems by Indian poet Sarojini Naidu; **Fragments of the Moon** (2013), poems by Italian poet Mario Rigli; **The Souls Dances in its Cradle** (2015), poems by Danish poet Niels Hav; all three translated into Arabic; **Contemporary Jordanian Poets, Volume I** (2013); **The Eyes of** *the Wind* (2014), poems by Tunisian poet Fadhila Masaai; ***The Birth of a Poet*** (2015), poems by Lebanese poet Mohammad Ikbal Harb. He is currently working on a translation project, **Arab Contemporary Poets Series**.

Sartawi's poems and translations have been anthologized and published in books, journals, and newspapers in Arab countries, the U.S., Australia, Indonesia, Italy, the Philippines, and India.

Inner Child Press

Inner Child Press is a Publishing Company Founded and Operated by Writers. Our personal publishing experiences provides us an intimate understanding of the sometimes daunting challenges Writers, New and Seasoned may face in the Business of Publishing and Marketing their Creative "Written Work".

For more Information

Inner Child Press

www.innerchildpress.com

intouch@innerchildpress.com

Made in the USA
San Bernardino, CA
30 April 2016